TRAVELLER

A CONFEDERATE GREY

TRAVELLER

A CONFEDERATE *GREY*

Photo courtesy of Library of Congress

THE WARHORSE OF ROBERT E. LEE

BEAU BURRIS

Library of Congress Control Number: 2005931367

ISBN: 1-59684-110-9

© 2005 Copyrights by Beau Burris
All Rights Reserved
Printed by *Derek Press*, Cleveland, TN

ACKNOWLEDGEMENTS

One day after some research on **Traveller**, I had a crazy idea about writing a book. Being naïve about the amount of work, time, and patience it takes to complete a project like this, I solicited help from Marcus Hand and Jerry Puckett of Derek Press. They both believed in the project from the start and encouraged my endeavor. In particular, Marcus Hand has gone above and beyond the scope of his duties. With his guidance and perseverance this book becomes possible. A special thanks to Wayne Slocumb of Derek Press for his work on the cover. I would also like to thank the many individuals who have helped me in my research and requisitioning of photographs. In particular, Vaughan Stanley and Lisa McCown at Washington and Lee University, Heather Milne at the Museum of the Confederacy, Judy Henson at Stratford Hall Plantation, Kenneth Johnson at the Library of Congress, Katie Lawhon at Gettysburg, Ed Jackson, and Don Troiani. A special thanks to Cindy Finnell for her assistance in editing and proofreading. Also, *thank you* for all the positive support from my friends and colleagues.

DEDICATION

To my father, who instilled in me an interest in history and a love for animals; to my mother, for her unending support in all things in life; to my wife, JoAnn, for her unconditional love; to my daughter, Summer, for indulging me in my efforts to teach her history (though it is really me that learns).

You are a Traveler, there will be many journeys.
—Chinese proverb—

FOREWORD

The relationship between humans and animals goes back to the beginning of time. Long before **Traveller** rode into General Lee's life, many species of animals had crossed the threshold of man's door and found a friendly hand to feed them. In return, they worked the fields, provided nourishment, and retrieved the prey. Often, the animal was the only confidant when all others had left.

Though I cannot give a first-hand account, I have attempted

to compile as much information about this veteran warhorse, using the available references that exist. We will never have the honor of petting the animal or shaking the General's hand, but this information gives us an idea of their life prior to legend. **Traveller**'s life was a short 14 years—but what a life he had. It is amazing how so many important events can unfold in such a short period of time; and yet life goes on.

This is a story about a horse that lived back some time ago. His most famous rider was a General in the Civil War and later became the President of a college. So why tell the story? Maybe it's because of inspiration. The inspiration to tell a story about history, and the inspiration to tell the story about an animal. What else provides the ability to get up every day and move forward; not backing down from a challenge and never living in the past, and always, *always* being loyal to those you love? This is the true story. The embodiment of these qualities makes the life of **Traveller** and General Robert E. Lee an inspiration for the rest of us. Their dedication to duty is honored, their loyalty admirable, and their story timeless.

CONTENTS

INTRODUCTION

On a memorable trip to Boston a few years ago, my family made a short stop in Lexington, Virginia. Since my father and I share a mutual interest in the history of the Civil War, we could not resist visiting Washington and Lee University, where General Robert E. Lee served as president in the years following the War. General Lee is entombed in the chapel on this campus.

When we were there a wedding was taking place, and we were unable to visit the tomb. A walk around the chapel provided interesting information, however, and one bit was a treasure.

BURIED NEAR THE GENERAL

We learned that **Traveller**, the legendary warhorse of General Lee, is buried just outside the chapel, near his beloved master. Since I am a self-proclaimed animal lover, I thought this was a special tribute to the horse. This incident sparked my interest in **Traveller**.

A small effort on my part to learn more about this equestrian hero yielded little information, so my interest sadly faded. Years later I returned to Lexington and decided to revisit the chapel.

Oddly, the chapel was closed again, and I was still unable to visit General Lee's tomb. But **Traveller** was there to greet me! This time I noticed two piles of pennies and an apple on his grave.

What did these gifts represent, and how can a horse spark such emotions in people over a century after his death? I vowed to answer these and other questions. As I began my research, I soon realized the stories and information were scattered among many different references. I thought it would be interesting to compile this information into one text.

This is a story about **Traveller**. I make no attempt to contemplate the Civil War. While it is true that one cannot truly appreciate the story without an appreciation of the times that frame this picture, **Traveller** did not know of a North or a South, Confederate or Union; nor could he analyze the different ideologies that overshadowed this country and divided a nation. To **Traveller**, it was only life.

To think about the horse, one has to wonder about the rider. **Traveller** was but a horse; the rider but a man. Together, they formed a legend, a legend that survives to this day. The two were brought together, survived a war, and buried at the same place.

MEMORIES OF TRAVELLER

The early times were hard; the retirement perhaps uneasy. It is easy to believe that they relied on each other. Probably more than we know.

Imagination easily sees the General mounted in battle, seated on his noble steed and overlooking a smoke-filled field. A more peaceful scene visualizes the lone General stroking the head of his steed, gently holding the reins, as a harvest moon shines through a canopy of trees. It is this kind of relationship between man and horse that brings this story to life.

This relationship begs to be told. **Traveller** was so recognized by the general public that Martha Custis "Markie" Williams, a famous artist of the day, wanted to paint a portrait of

Traveller. Lee's daughter, Agnes, was the widow of the artist's son, so she relayed the request to Lee. The general wrote this letter to Agnes:

> If I were an artist like you, I would draw a picture of Traveller—representing his fine proportions, muscular figure, deep chest and short back, strong haunches, flat legs, small head, broad forehead, delicate ears, quick eye, small feet, and black mane and tail. Such a picture would inspire a poet, whose genius could then depict his worth and describe his endurance of toil, hunger, thirst, heat, cold, and the dangers and sufferings through which he passed. He could dilate upon his sagacity and affection, and his invariable response to every wish of his rider. He might even imagine his thoughts, through the long night marches and days of battle through which he has passed.
>
> But I am no artist; I can only say he is a Confederate grey.

"GEN. LEE on TRAVELLER."

Photo courtesy of Library of Congress

1

ALL THE KING'S HORSES

A witness who saw General Robert E. Lee astride his famous warhorse, described both like this:

I saw [Lee] once on **Traveller. Traveller** moved as if proud of the burden he bore. To me, the horse was beautiful and majestic. It was the only time I was impressed with the greatness and beauty and power and glory of the man. He

Photo courtesy of Library of Congress

sat erect in the saddle. The gloved hand held the bridle, the other hung gracefully at his side. He was every inch a king.

It is not difficult to think of this regal horse as fit for a king, for in a day when the horse was essential for transportation and everyday life, **Traveller** stood out. Nor is it difficult for us to understand the importance of a good horse in the Civil War.

Although **Traveller** became General Lee's most notable horse, the Lee family owned several horses. Perhaps we will never know just how many mounts he really owned. While living in Baltimore prior to the Civil War, Lee presented his son with a mustang pony named **Santa Anna**. This horse had been ridden by Jim Connally, a man who served with him in the war with Mexico. The pony was pure white in color, and stood about 14 hands high.

In Baltimore, **Santa Anna** and **Grace Darling**, described as Lee's favorite mare, were considered members of the Lee family. **Santa Anna** was found dead in a park in Arlington, Virginia, in the winter of 1860-1861.

Grace Darling was a chestnut of fine size and possessed great power. Lee bought this mare in Texas on his way to the war with Mexico in 1847. She became available when her owner died on the long march. In the spring of 1863, **Grace Darling** was confiscated by a federal quartermaster when General McClellan occupied Lee's home in Arlington, Virginia (now the site of Arlington National Cemetery). The General was in western Virginia at the time, commanding the Army of Virginia.

A gentleman from Richmond presented Lee with a bay stallion in the spring of 1861. The General rode this horse when he inspected the Richmond defenses, so he named him **Richmond**. After the Battle of Malvern Hill in 1862, Richmond died.

Brown Roan was purchased by Lee in western Virginia during the first summer of the war. Also referred to as **The Roan**, the horse went blind in 1862 and had to be retired. He was given to a farmer.

Photo courtesy of Library of Congress

LUCY LONG

Two other horses, **Ajax** and **Lucy Long**, joined Lee's stable after he purchased **Traveller. Lucy Long**, a mare, served as the primary backup horse to **Traveller. Lucy Long** remained with the Lee family after the war was over. Outliving General Lee, she died when she was 33 years old. The following account of **Lucy Long**, the lesser known warhorse of General Lee, appeared in the *Abington Virginian* on February 13, 1891:

There have appeared from time to time during the past year announcements in Southern newspapers of war-horses ridden during the war by some Confederate soldier, with the caption, "The Last War-horse of the Confederacy," or something similar.

It will be learned, doubtless with surprise by some, that there is yet living and in good health, save for the infirmities common to old age, a horse ridden in battle during the war by General Robert E. Lee. It is **Lucy Long**, a little sorrel mare, which many will recall having seen ladies ride through the streets of Lexington alongside of General Lee astride of his more famous warhorse, **Traveller**.

Lucy Long was a present to General Lee from General J. E. B. Stuart in 1862, when the former was conducting the Sharpsburg campaign. That summer George Lee was standing in a skirmish line holding **Traveller**. The horse was high-spirited, impatient and hard to hold and pulled the General down a steep bank and broke his hands. For a time he found it necessary to travel in an ambulance. It was then that General Stuart found **Lucy Long**, bought her and gave her to him.

She was a low, easy-moving, and quiet sorrel mare. General Stuart purchased her from Mr. Stephen Dandridge, the owner of 'The Bower,' a country place in Jefferson county famous in that day for its hospitality and a famous resort of Stuart with his staff, when in that locality.

General Lee rode **Lucy Long** for two years until, when in the lines around Petersburg, she got with foal, and he sent her to the rear, and once more mounted **Traveller**. She was stolen just before the close of the war, and after the surrender was found in the eastern part of the State, and Captain R. E. Lee brought her to Lexington to his father.

Photo courtesy of Library of Congress

Several years after General Lee's death, and possibly thirteen years ago, while running at large in the grounds in the rear of the University, by some unknown means **Lucy Long** got the leaders of her hind legs cut. She was henceforth of no service, and General Custis Lee got the late John Riplogle, the greatest horse lover in Rockbridge in his day, to be responsible for her and take charge of her on his farm in Buffalo.

On Mr. Riplogle's death, a few years ago, she was turned over to the care of Mr. John R. Mackay, who lives in the same neighborhood, and there she is at this time. When purchased by General Stuart she was said to be five years old. She is probably now in her thirty-fourth year.

Lucy Long is thin in flesh, though her eyes have not lost their wonted brightness and her health apparently is good. She eats dry food with difficulty, hence her present condition.

During the grazing season she fattens on the soft grasses
of the pasture.

LEE'S MOUNTS

A gentlemen of southwest Virginia presented to General Lee
Ajax, a sorrel horse, but he was used infrequently because he was
too large for Lee to ride comfortably. He remained with the Lees
after the war, and was killed in the mid-1860s by accidently running into the prong of an iron gate latch. He is also buried on the
grounds of Washington and Lee University.

Lee compared his other mounts to **Traveller** by saying that of
all his companions in toil, **Richmond, Brown Roan, Ajax,**
and quiet **Lucy Long, Traveller** was the only horse that retained his vigor to the end.

The first two expired under their onerous burden, and the last
two failed in old age. Other famous horses of the Civil War are
worth mentioning. I have listed some notable warhorses and their
famous riders, both Confederate and Union, in Appendix 1.

2

AKA TRAVELLER

Traveller was born in 1857 in Greenbrier County near the White Sulphur Springs, now in West Virginia. Attempts to link **Traveller's** bloodlines to Virginia's registrable horses have been unsuccessful. Still, Fairfax Harrison, the chronicler of Virginia's famous equines, concluded that "circumstantial as well as physical evidence was persuasive that however derived, the horse (**Traveller**) was 'bred'."

Even though his lineage cannot be documented, from the beginning **Traveller** gave evidence of being a splendid animal. He was first called **Jeff Davis** by Andrew Johnston, who raised him. **Traveller** took first prizes at the Lewisburg fairs for both 1859 and 1860.

When the horse was three years old, Johnston presented him to his son, J.W.Johnston. At the outset of the Civil War, the younger Johnston rode **Jeff Davis** during the western Virginia campaign. During these operations, Lee first saw the horse. He immediately inquired about the steed, only to learn that Johnston had promised to sell him to Captain Joseph M.Broun. Broun wanted him for his brother, Major Thomas L. Broun.

> When the Wise legion was encamped on Sewell mountain, opposing the advance of the Federal Army under Rosecranz, in the fall of 1861, I was Major (Thomas L. Broun) to the Third regiment of infantry in that legion, and my brother, Captain Joseph M. Broun, was quartermaster to

Photo courtesy of Library of Congress

the same regiment. I authorized my brother to purchase a good serviceable horse of the best Greenbrier stock for our use during the war. After much inquiry and search he came across the horse (**Traveller**), and I purchased him for $175 (gold value), from Captain James W. Johnston.

When the Wise legion was encamped about Meadow Bluff and Big Sewell mountains, I rode this horse, which was greatly admired in camp for his rapid, springy walk, his high spirit, bold carriage, and his muscular strength. He needed neither whip nor spur, and would walk his five or six miles an hour over the rough mountain roads of Western Virginia with his rider sitting firmly in the saddle and holding him in check by a tight rein, such vim and eagerness did he manifest to go right ahead so soon as he was mounted.

When General Lee took command of the Wise Legion and Floyd Brigade encamped near the Big Sewell mountains, in the fall of 1861, he first saw the horse, and took a great fancy to it. He always referred to him as my colt and he let the Broun brothers know of his continuing interest in the animal.

Photo courtesy of Library of Congress

Late in 1861, as winter approached, the climate in West Virginia mountains caused Rosecranz's army to abandon its position on the Big Sewell and retreat westward. General Lee was thereupon ordered to South Carolina. The Third regiment of the Wise legion was subsequently detached from the army in Western Virginia, and ordered to the South Carolina coast, where it was known as the Sixtieth Virginia regiment, under Colonel Starke.

In a short time Joseph M. Broun arrived riding **Jeff Davis**, whose name had apparently been changed to **Greenbrier**. Thomas L. Broun had remained in western Virginia, because he was ill. General Lee at once recognized the horse, and again inquired of him pleasantly about 'his colt'. My brother then offered him the horse as a gift, which the General promptly declined. At the same time he remarked: "If you will willingly sell me the horse, I will gladly use it for a week or so to learn its qualities." Thereupon my brother had the horse sent to General Lee's stable.

In about a week the horse was returned to my brother, with a note from General Lee stating that the animal suited him, but that he could no longer use so valuable a horse in such times, unless it was his own; that if he (my brother) would not sell, please to keep the horse, with many thanks. This was in February, 1862. At that time I was in Virginia, on the sick list from a long and severe attack of camp fever, contracted in the campaign on Big Sewell mountains.

My brother wrote me of General Lee's desire to have the horse, and asked me what he should do. I replied: "If he will not accept it, then sell it to him at what is cost me." He then sold the horse to General Lee for $200 in currency, the sum of $25 added by General Lee to the price I paid for the horse in September, 1861, to make up the depreciation in our currency from September, 1861, to February, 1862.

In 1868 General Lee wrote to my brother, stating that this horse had survived the war, and was known as **Traveller** (spelling the word with a double l in good English style). He was asking for its pedigree, which was obtained, and sent by my brother to General Lee.

General Lee renamed the animal because of its pluck and energy. **Traveller** weighed around eleven hundred pounds and stood 15.3 hands high. He was iron-gray with black points mane and tail, very dark.

Traveller was not only iron-grey in color, but iron in constitution, and was Lee's favorite mount. Some think the horse was an ambler (like a Tennessee Walking Horse), but no facts exist to prove that. His conformation does seem to resemble the Plantation Horse, which had an ambling gait.

Captain Lee wrote of **Traveller**, "He was never known to tire, and, though quiet and sensible in general and afraid of nothing, yet if not regularly exercised, he fretted a good deal, especially in a crowd of horses. After the war, a Lexington resident, who often saw Lee riding **Traveller**, observed that **Traveller** was a "mighty proud horse," and added, "he looked like just the horse for General Lee."

Traveller and Lee. As a pair they were a symbol of indestructibility, a reassuring quality that existed outside the mutations of time and circumstance.

3

MEETING
THE GENERAL

Among the soldiers in the southern army, this horse was as well known as his master. Someone has said: "But to fully know the horse, one must also understand his master. Both were respected by all who knew them, and the two became inseparable in relentless battle, in heartbreaking defeat and in signal honor."

Robert Edward Lee was born on January 19, 1807, at Stratford in Westmoreland County, Virginia. He was the fifth child born to Henry "Light-Horse Harry" Lee and his second wife, Ann Hill (Carter) Lee. Robert had many ties to Revolutionary War heroes. He grew up in an area where George Washington was still a living memory.

Educated in the Alexandria, Virginia, schools, he obtained an appointment to West Point in 1825. In 1829, Robert E. Lee graduated second in his class without a single demerit against his name. He served as the cadet corps' adjutant. His classmates dubbed him the "Marble Statue" for his nearly perfect record while at the academy.

Lee was commissioned a brevet 2nd Lieutenant in the Corps of Engineers. On June 30, 1831, he married Mary Ann Randolph Custis. Her mother was Mary Custis of Arlington, the wife of Mr. Washington Custis, the grandson of George and

Martha Washington. Together, Lee and Mary Custis had seven children. All three of their sons served in the Confederate army. Both George Washington Custis and William Henry Fitzhugh "Rooney" attained the rank of Major General. Robert E. Lee, Jr. attained the rank of Captain. He was a private in the Rockbridge Artillery at the Battle of Antietam.

Before the Mexican War, Robert E. Lee served on engineering projects in Georgia, Virginia and New York. During that war with Mexico, he served on the staffs of both John Wool and Winfield Scott. Because of his gallantry and distinguished conduct in performing vital scouting missions, he was promoted to Colonel.

Following a stint in Baltimore Harbor in 1852, he became Superintendent of the United States Military Academy at West Point, where he held the prestigious post with distinction. In 1855, Secretary of War Jefferson Davis transferred Lee from staff to line and commissioned him Lieutenant Colonel in the

Second Cavalry. With gratitude he accepted the promotion because of the painfully slow promotions in the engineers' corps.

Ordered to western Texas, he served with his regiment until the 1857 death of his father-in-law forced him to ask for a series of leaves in order to settle the estate.

In 1859, Lee was assigned to lead the force of marines that put down John Brown's raid on Harper's Ferry in western Virginia. After this, he was re-assigned to Texas, where he served until he was summoned to Washington in 1861 by General Winfield Scott. By now, several states in the South had already seceded from the Union. Scott, who was Lee's commander in Mexico, tried to persuade Lee to remain loyal in the service of the United States.

He was offered the command of the Union's field forces on the day after Virginia seceded, and two days after the initial

offer from Scott. In a letter to his sister, dated April 20, 1861,
Lee wrote:

> With all my devotion to the Union and the feeling of loyalty
> and duty of an American citizen, I have not been able to make
> up my mind to raise my hand against my relatives, my chil-
> dren, my home. I have therefore, resigned my commission
> in the Army, and save in defense of my native State, with the
> sincere hope that my poor services may never be needed, I
> hope I may never be called on to draw my sword.

His resignation was accepted on April 25, 1861. He then
accepted an invitation to visit Governor John Letcher in Virginia. Politically, Robert E. Lee was a Whig. Ironically, while
he was attached strongly to the Union and to the Constitution,
he entertained no special sympathy for slavery.

Lee proceeded to Richmond, the capital of the Confederacy,
and was named Commander-in-Chief of the military and
naval forces of Virginia. Now in charge of Virginia's fledgling
military might, he became involved primarily in organizational

matters. As a Confederate brigadier general (later a full general), he was in charge of supervising all Southern forces operating in Virginia.

In the first summer of the war, Lee was assigned his first field command in western Virginia. The Cheat Mountain Campaign was a disappointing fizzle, due largely to the failings of his superiors. His entire tenure in the region was unpleasant because he had to put up with the petty bickering of his subordinates. The offending underlings included William W. Loring, John B. Floyd and Henry A. Wise.

After this, Lee became known throughout the South as "Granny Lee."

His debut in field command had not been promising but Jefferson Davis, now President of the Confederacy, appointed him to command the forces along the Southern Coast. In March of 1862, Lee became a military advisor to President Davis.

In this position he had some influence over military operations, especially those of Stonewall Jackson in the Shenandoah Valley. When Joseph E. Johnston launched his attack at Seven Pines, Davis and Lee were taken by surprise and rode out to the field. In the confusion of the fight Johnston was badly wounded. That night Davis relieved the wounded Johnston, and appointed Lee to take command.

Lee promptly renamed the the troops the Army of Northern Virginia. He led the fighting on the second day, but the initiative had already been lost. Later in the month, in a surprisingly daring move, Lee left a small force guarding Richmond, and crossed the Chickahominy to strike the Union forces north of the river.

In what came to be called the Seven Days Battles, the individual fights at Beaver Dam Creek, Gaines' Mill, Savage Station, Glendale, White Oak Swamp and Malvern Hill were actually tactical defeats for the Confederates. Lee, however, achieved the strategic goal of dislodging McClellan's army from the very gates of Richmond. The Union forces began a retreat back toward Washington, D.C. This all created a new opinion of Lee in the South. Gradually, He came to be known as "Uncle Robert" and "Marse Robert."

With McClellan neutralized, a new threat developed under John Pope in northern Virginia. Lee first detached Jackson and then followed with Longstreet's command winning this strategic battle at Second Bull Run, Lee moved on into Maryland but he suffered the misfortune of having a copy of his orders fall into the hands of the enemy.

Seeing Lee's forces divided and his strategy betrayed, McClellan moved with unusual speed to engage him. Lee was forced to fight a delaying action along South Mountain while waiting for Jackson to complete the capture of Harper's Ferry and rejoin him. Still, he masterfully fought McClellan to a standstill at Antietam; and two days later, recrossed the Potomac River.

Near the end of the year, he won an easy victory over Burnside at Fredericksburg. Then he trounced Hooker in his most creditable victory to date at Chancellorsville, where he executed a brilliant tactical movement. He

GENERAL ROBERT E. LEE

Photo courtesy of Library of Congress

detached Jackson with most of the army on a lengthy flank march, while remaining in the immediate front of the Union army with only two divisions.

Launching his second invasion of the North, Lee lost at Gettysburg. On the third day of this battle he displayed one of his major faults. At Malvern Hill, as well as on other fields, he had ordered a massed infantry assault across a wide open plain, not recognizing that the rifle was subjecting the charging troops to withering fire for too long a period at the time.

The rifle had come into use since the Mexican War. Another persistent problem with which Lee had to cope was his subordinates' failure to execute with dispatch the general orders he issued.

Returning to Virginia after Gettysburg, General Lee was the commander in the inconclusive Bristoe and Mine Run Campaigns. From the Wilderness to Petersburg he fought a retiring campaign against Grant in which he made full use of entrenchments. His tactics earned him yet another sobriquet—"Ace of Spades Lee."

Although he was named Commander in Chief of the Confederate Armies on January 23, 1865, Robert E. Lee nevertheless found himself too occupied in Virginia to give more than general directives to the theaters of war in other states.

Richmond was finally forced into a siege. Lee held the city, however, as well as Petersburg, for nearly 10 months before beginning his retreat to Appomattox. There, he would be forced to cede the inevitable.

On April 9, 1865, General Lee surrendered to General Ulysses S. Grant at a little village called Appomattox Court House. He returned to Richmond as a paroled prisoner of war. It was not until August 5, 1975, 110 years after General Lee's application, that President Gerald R. Ford signed Joint Resolution

23, restoring the long overdue full rights of citizenship to General Robert E. Lee.

Lee's farewell to the Army of Northern Virginia is a classic. Lee said:

> After four years of arduous service, marked by unsurpassed courage and fortitude, the Army of Northern Virginia has been compelled to yield to overwhelming numbers and resources.
>
> I need not tell the survivors of so many hard-fought battles who have remained steadfast to the last that I have consented to this result from no distrust of them; but feeling that valor and devotion could accomplish nothing that could compensate for the loss that would have attended the continuance of the contest, I determined to avoid the useless sacrifice of those whose past services have endeared them to their countrymen.
>
> By the terms of the agreement, officers and men can return to their homes and remain until exchanged.
>
> You may take with you the satisfaction that proceeds from the consciousness of duty faithfully performed, and I earnestly

pray that a merciful God will extend to you his blessing and protection.

With an unceasing admiration of your constancy and devotion to your country, and a grateful remembrance of your kind and generous consideration of myself, I bid you all an affectionate farewell.

4

CHARGING HELL

Traveller was involved in many battles of the war. In fact, everytime you see a picture of General Lee on a horse it is Traveller. Here are a few accounts of Traveller and Lee in battle. In referring to Traveller, Lee stated:

> I purchased him in the mountains of Virginia in the autumn of 1861, and he has been my patient follower ever since—to Georgia, the Carolinas, and back to Virginia. He carried me through the Seven Days Battle; around

Richmond; the Second Manassas; Sharpburg; Fredericksburg; the last day at Chancellorsville; to Pennsylvania,
at Gettysburg;, and back to the Rappahannock. From the
commencement of the campaign in 1864 at Orange, till its
close around Petersburg, the saddle was scarcely off his back,
as he passed through the fire of the Wilderness, Spottsylvania,
Cold Harbour, and across the James River.

He was almost in daily requisition in the winter of 1864-65
on the long line of defenses from Chickahominy, north of
Richmond, to Hatcher's Run, south of the Appomattox.
In the campaign of 1865, he bore me from Petersburg to
the final days at Appomattox Court House. You must
know the comfort he is to me.

Around 3:30 A.M., on May 6, 1864, Confederate Gen. Cad-
mus M. Wilcox was alarmed that reinforcements led by Gen.
James Longstreet had not yet reached the Wilderness. The Union
forces broke through the Confederate center line of defenses,
and panic-stricken Southerners ran from the lines, singly at
first and then in clusters of eight to a dozen.

As General John Gregg's Texans hurried to plug the hole, a worried Lee raised himself in his stirrups, uncovered his gray hair and exclaimed in front of the whole command, "Texans always move them."

> Never before in my lifetime did I ever see a such a scene that was enacted when Lee pronounced these words, a yell rang in the air that must have been heard from miles around, a courier riding by my side with tears running

"Lee's Texans" by Don Troiani

down his cheeks exclaimed, "I would charge hell itself for that old man."

Soon Longstreet's reinforcements arrived. The new arrivals formed a line of battle close to their gun pits and prepared for a countercharge. As the infantry started forward, Lee guided **Traveller** into the line and spurred the animal forward.

When the Texans realized what was happening, spontaneous shouts went up. Ignoring frantic warnings to go back, Lee was obsessed, and acted as though he had heard nothing. Some said, "His face was aflame and his eyes were on the enemy in the front."

Gregg tried and failed to turn **Traveller's** head. At a signal from Gregg, however, a sergeant seized the bridle rein of Lee's horse, and this action slowed **Traveller**. Still Lee continued to move toward the head of the line until Col. Charles S. Venable rode to his side, shouting,

"Longstreet has arrived!" Lee reined his animal back, and appeared to return to his normal countenance. This action soon gave rise to a host of oral accounts and a poem titled, *Lee to the Rear!* by John R. Thompson. The bard wrote:

The grand old gray-beard rode to the space

Where Death and his victims stood face to face.

On a drizzly Thursday morning, May 12, 1864, reinforcements arrived for the Battle of Spotslyvania. As they arrived, the drizzle turned into rain and the brigade, having hurried through the mud from across the river, halted briefly on the courthouse road directly behind the open base of the salient. General Lee rode to the head of the column on his gray horse, **Traveller**, and called to Nat Harris's Mississippians to move rapidly to Commander Rode's assistance.

This time there was no indication or suggestion that the General intended to lead the troops into battle. In his urgency to hurry the men, he was riding at the head of the column beside General Harris, when their line of march came under sudden artillery fire. **Traveller** reared. While his forefeet clawed the air, a solid shot passed under the horse's belly and barely missed taking off Lee's stirrup. Although Lee frequently commanded in a dangerous field of fire, this was the only recorded incident when he had such a close brush with death or maiming.

Lee Park, Dallas Texas

Frightened soldiers yelled, "Go back, General Lee! For God's sake, go back!"

At Chancellorsville, from their first sight of the erect, immaculate, utterly calm, gray-bearded man riding that unmistakable gray warhorse toward the burning Chancellor house, the soldiers of his Army of Northern Virginia seemed to forget everything they had just endured and broke into wild cheering.

Eagerly the war-weary soldiers thronged him, brushing **Traveller's** flanks, ignoring the frantic cries of staff officers to let the General pass so that he and they could get on with the battle. But the tumultuous and triumphant shouting continued, with General Lee as composed in the midst of it as he had been during the worst moments of any battle.

"It must have been from such a scene," wrote an observer later, "that men in ancient time rose to the dignity of gods." The General's son, Captain Lee, remembered

> being present when that of the Third Army Corps, General A. P. Hill commanding, a review of the Army of Northern Virginia took place. Some of us young cavalrymen, then stationed near the Rappahannock, rode over to Orange Court House to see this grand military pageant.

From all parts of the army, officers and men who could get leave came to look on, and from all the surrounding country the people, old and young, ladies and children, came in every pattern of vehicle and on horseback, to see twenty thousand of that incomparable infantry of the Army of Northern Virginia pass in review before their great commander.

The General was mounted on **Traveller**, who looked proud of his master. [The General] had on sash and sword, which he rarely wore, a pair of new cavalry gauntlets and a new hat. He looked unusually fine, and sat his horse like a perfect picture of grace and power.

The infantry was drawn up in column by divisions, with their bright muskets all glittering in the sun, their battleflags standing straight out before the breeze, and their bands playing, awaiting the inspection of the General, before they broke into column by companies and marched past him in review.

When all was ready, General Hill and staff rode up to General Lee; and the two generals, with their respective staffs, galloped around front and rear of each of the three divisions standing motionless on the plain. As the cavalcade reached the head of each division, its commanding officer joined in and followed as far as the next division, so that there was a continual infusion of fresh groups into the original one all along the lines.

Traveller started with a long lope, and never changed his stride. His rider sat erect and calm, not noticing anything but the gray lines of men whom he knew so well. The pace was very fast, as there were nine good miles to go, and the escort began to become less and less, dropping out

"Brandy Station Review" by Don Troiani

one by one from different causes as **Traveller** raced along without a check.

When the General drew up—after this nine-mile gallop—under the standard at the reviewing-stand, flushed with the exercise as well as with pride in his brave men, he raised his hat and saluted. Then arose a shout of applause and admiration from the entire assemblage, the memory of which to this day moistens the eye of every old soldier.

A HORSE NAMED TRAVELLER

Captain Robert E. Lee tells a story about himself and **Traveller**. In the winter of 1862, his father broke his hands in the Battle of Second Manassas, and the younger Lee was asked to ride **Traveller** from Orange to Fredericksburg.

Having just been promoted to the cavalry, the young Captain needed the additional regimen, and especially this kind of riding experience.

So I mounted with some misgivings, though I was very proud of my steed. My misgivings were fully realized, for **Traveller** would not walk at all. He took a short, high trot a buck-trot, as compared with a buck jump and kept it up to Fredericksburg, some 30 miles away.

Although young, strong and tough, I was glad when the journey ended. This was my first introduction to the cavalry service. I think I am safe in saying that I could have walked the distance with much more comfort and less fatigue.

GEN ROBT E. LEE

Photo courtesy of Library of Congress

McLean and Appomattox

A Virginian by the name of Wilbur McLean had allowed Generals Johnston and Beauregard to use his house a few miles east of Manassas as a temporary headquarters back in 1861. Then he saw it destroyed by federal gunfire on the day of the war's first major battle. So McLean had moved his family to a place so far from the fighting he thought danger could not follow. He had moved them to the little village called Appomattox Court House.

Photo courtesy of Library of Congress

Now, almost four years later, the war had caught up with him again. Lee had sent Colonel Walter Marshall to select an appropriate place for the dreaded but inevitable meeting with Grant.Colonel Marshall went to Wilburn McLean who showed him an empty building. The Colonel rejected it. Curiously, McLean did not suggest either the courthouse or a brick tavern nearby, but he did offer his own house.

Around midday on Palm Sunday, April 9, 1864, General Lee dismounted and handed **Traveller's** reins to Sergeant G. W. Tucker, who led the gray horse over to graze on McLean's lawn. The surrender took place in the McLean's parlor. It read:

In accordance with the substance of my letter to you of the 8th instant, I propose to receive the surrender of the Army of Northern Virginia on the following terms, to wit:

Rolls of all the officers and men to be made in duplicate, one copy to be given to an officer designated by me, the other to be retained by such officer or officers as you may designate.

The officers to give their individuals paroles not to take up arms against the Government of the United States until properly exchanged; and each company or regimental commander to sign a like parole for the men of their commands.

The arms, artillery and public property to be parked and stacked, and turned over to the officers appointed by me to receive them. This will not embrace the side-arms of the officers, nor their private horses or baggage.

This done, each officer and man will be allowed to return to his home, not to be disturbed by U.S. authority so long as they observe their paroles and the laws in force where they may reside.

"This will have a very happy effect on my army," said Lee, as he returned the text to General Grant. And well may he have made such a comment, for Grant's closing sentence was, in effect, amnesty—assurance that they would not be prosecuted for treason.

There was one problem, however, and Lee raised it. Horses used by cavalrymen and artillerymen were the individual soldiers' property, not the Confederate government's. "I will instruct the officers I shall appoint to receive the paroles," said Grant, "to let all the men who claim to own a horse or mule to take the animals home with them to work their little farms."

General Lee was pleased with the generous terms of surrender. He added that this would go far toward conciliating our people. Lee stepped out to the porch and received **Traveller's** reins from

Tucker. Now he could see General Grant standing on McLean's porch, his hat raised.

Lee raised his hat in a return salute, then nudged **Traveller** toward legendary status.

Photo courtesy of Library of Congress

5

PORTRAIT
OF A HORSE

GENERAL LEE AND TRAVELLER

By Rev. Robert Tuttle

Behold that horse! A dappled gray!
I saw him in the month of May,
When wild flowers bloomed about his feet,
And sunshine was his mantle meet.

The shapely head he held up high,
And fire seemed flashing from his eye;
Arched grandly, too, his neck and mane,
And on them fell the slackened rein.

Down from the withers to the tail
The curve was perfect in detail,
While depth of chest, and haunch, and side,
Showed where his strength did most reside.

Monument Avenue Richmond, Virginia courtesy of Virginia Tourism Corp

Photo by Ed Jackson

With limb, and hoof, and pastern small,
The body round and plump withal,
No pattern could be perfecter
Than was the form of **Traveller.**

Rare model for an artist's skill!
For brush, or chisel, or for quill!
For there, with muscles strained and tense,
His mould was sheer magnificence.

Bucephalus was not more gay
In ancient battle's stern array,
Than was that grand Virginia gray,
That mutely champed his bits that day.

A day of battle, truly, then!
A day of death to many men!
For war a gory drama played
But **"Traveller"** was undismayed.

Dismounted, and quite near his head,
The right hand to the halter wed,
His rider stood, bold leader he!
The great, the gallant Robert Lee.

Broad shouldered, tall, stout, and straight,
The left hand down, his look sedate,
He wore a cap and suit of gray
And gazed, but nothing had to say.

What courtliness in him was seen!
Aye, what nobility of mien!
As there, Horatius-like, he stood
The honored, wise, and great, and good.

Great Chieftains had preceded him
With cups of glory to the brim,
But he among them all was Prince,
Unrivalled in the past, or since.

The battle raged around him near;
The clash of arms he saw, could hear,
But, dauntless, he stood out to view,
Though deadly missiles round him flew.

Brave Chief and Charger! Such were they.
In Dixie's hue of martial gray,
And such they will in memory be,
While time and sense remain to me.

Immortal Spottsylvania!
Twas on that sacred hill of thine,
Mid shouts of victory and huzzah,
We saw this picture from the line.

Ye artists! Paint the signal scene
Or fashion it in bronze, or stone,
That generations, yet unseen,
In all our Southland's sunny zone,

May look upon Lee's noble form,
As there he stood amid the storm,
And did our Dixie Boys command,
Who fought for rights, and home, and land.

No need have we for Northern foe,
Living, or dead, above, below;
We honor those who wore the gray,
And weave for them our last bouquet.

We War's arbitrament accept,
And foemen leave in peace to rest,
But, when their graves are decked and wept.
The North must do it, and Northwest.

Away with sickly sentiment!
True Southrons never will repent;
For "Chartered Rights," they fought the fight,
And still they know their cause was right.

Photo courtesy of Washington and Lee University

6

THE WAR ENDS

After the war, when Lee was president of Washington College in Lexington, Virginia, a friend saw him pause in a ride down a Lexington street to greet a woman friend on the sidewalk. Lee sat on **Traveller** with his hat and reins in one hand, graciously making small-talk.

As they met, **Traveller** reared on hind legs several times and came to earth in response to Lee's tugs.

Unaccountably, **Traveller** continued to rear throughout the interview, a mystery to all except the observant friend across the street. He could see the General as he slyly dug the horse with his left spur, using the occasion to indulge a small vanity over his horsemanship.

After the war, General Lee looked toward the future. He had always wanted a small farm, because he felt that life in Richmond was not suited to him. In the first days of June, he rode down to Pampatike, a plantation owned by Colonel Thomas H. Carter.

While he rested, his company observed how good it was to see **Traveller** enjoying himself. Lee had turned the majestic warhorse out on the lawn where the June grass was fine, abundant and at its prime. The caring general would allow no corn to be fed to **Traveller**, saying he had had plenty of that during

Photo courtesy of Virginia Tourism Corp

the last four years. He remarked that the grass and liberty were what he needed. As the visit ended, someone observed:

> **Traveller** was brought up to the door for him to mount, he walked all around him, looking carefully at the horse, saddle and bridle. Apparently, the blanket was not arranged to suit him, for he held the bridle while Uncle Henry took off the saddle.
>
> Then he took off the blanket himself, spread it out on the grass, and, folding it to suit his own ideas of fitness, carefully placed it on **Traveller's** back, and superintended closely the putting on and girthing of the saddle. This being done, he bade everybody good-bye, mounted his horse, and rode away homeward to Richmond.

Lee spent the rest of the summer in Derwent, near Cartersville, Virginia. **Traveller** was in constant use as the General made several excursions to friends and family. It was during this period that he wrote of riding "the gray" in reference to **Traveller**. That summer proved to be a welcome relaxation from the war years.

COLLEGE PRESIDENT

Lee was offered the vice-chancellorship of the University of the South at Sewanee, Tennessee; but he declined because of its denominational status. Shortly afterward, he was offered the presidency of Washington College, and he accepted.

This university had opened in 1749 and was the first classical school opened in the Valley of Virginia. General George Washington had noted the college and awarded it a handsome endowment.

As a result, the institution changed its name from "Libery Hall Academy" to Washington College.

The college had suffered from the ravages of war, and at the time, had only four professors and about 40 students. It was not an institution supported by the state, nor was it confined to any a single religious denomination. After the board of trustees had satisfied Lee's many apprehensions, he accepted the offer.

General Lee mounted **Traveller** and began the journey to Lexington. Only the two made the journey. They arrived in Lexington on September 24. On September 14, 1865, Mary Curtis Lee, had written a friend:

> He starts tomorrow en cheval for Lexington. He prefers that way; and, besides, does not like to part even for a time from his beloved steed, the companion of many a hard-fought battle.

Lee took the oath of office at Washington College on October 2, 1865. His wife did not join him because of an illness. Also, the college was preparing a house for his family.

Lee wrote lovingly of his fondness for his famous horse that people always remarked about when they saw him:

> **Traveller** is my only companion; I may also say my pleasure. He and I, whenever practicable, wander out in the mountains and enjoy sweet confidence. The boys are plucking out his tail, and he is presenting the appearance of a plucked chicken.

Lee and **Traveller** met their family on December 2, and escorted them to the home at Lexington. With his family now with him, the General now began focusing on his duties to the college. He began forming strong relationships with the students and improving the facilities.

It was Lee's desire to keep himself from undue public attention. He often dismissed requests for interviews about the war.

During the next summer, Lee often rode **Traveller** to the Warm Springs bath. They made the trip about once a week, stopping along the way to visit with his neighbors. Little children along the route soon became acquainted with the gray horse and his stately rider.

WITH THE WAR FAR AWAY

On December 22, 1866, his son, Captain Lee, arrived for Christmas with **Lucy Long** in tow. The General had reimbursed the man who had purchased her from someone who had no right to her. Now, the General was usually accompanied on his rides on **Traveller** by one of his daughters.

The General would usually saddle **Traveller** about 4:00 p.m. each day and take a long ride. Sometimes he would ride as much as 20 miles. Lee often gave **Traveller** what he called a breather, allowing the horse to gallop at full speed for a time. Afterward, he would settle down to a calm walk.

Captain Lee, the son, began to ride **Traveller** more and more. The General was occupied in putting behind him such scenes as the long ride from Orange to Fredericksburg in the winter of 1862. One summer he wrote a letter to his clerk in Lexington from the Springs. In it he asked:

> How is **Traveller**? Tell him I miss him dreadfully, and have repented of our separation but once—and that is the whole time since we parted.

Captain Lee wrote his own memoirs years later. In his narrative, he said:

> I think **Traveller** appreciated his love and sympathy, and returned it as much as was in a horse's nature to do. He was allowed the freedom of the college grounds. The faculty houses had fenced yards to prevent damage to vegetable and flower gardens; but at the Lee home, **Traveller** was allowed within the fence.

> Students recalled that **Traveller** always saluted his master with a toss of his head when Lee entered the yard. They remembered that Lee indulged the horse with sugar lumps,

and sometimes just stood quietly watching his beautiful animal.

One July afternoon, the General rode down to the canal-boat landing to put on board a young lady who had been visiting his daughters. The General dismounted, tied **Traveller** to a post, and was standing on the boat making his adieux, when some one called out that **Traveller** was loose.

Sure enough, the gallant gray was making his way up the road, increasing his speed as he went. A number of boys and men were trying to stop him. My father immediately stepped ashore, called to the crowd to stand still, and advancing a few steps gave a peculiar low whistle. At the first sound, **Traveller** stopped and pricked up his ears.

The General whistled a second time, and the horse with a glad whinny turned and trotted quietly back to his master, who patted and coaxed him before tying him up again. To a bystander expressing surprise at the creature's docility, the General observed that he did not see how any man could ride a horse for any length of time without a perfect understanding being established between them.

The General would often give rides to children around his home. These rides were considered the greatest treat the General could offer. On one of these rides, a picture of Lee's lighter side was revealed. "Come with me, little girls, and I will show you a beautiful ride," he said.

Only too delighted, they consented to go. One of them had her face tied up, as she was just recovering from the mumps. He pretended that he was much alarmed lest his horse should catch them from her, and kept saying: I hope you won't give **Traveller** the mumps! and "What shall I do if **Traveller** gets the mumps?"

Traveller was observed as stepping very proudly with his young riders aboard.

Lee would often ride high into the mountains, sometimes with others and sometimes alone. He was very fond of horseback journeys, enjoyed the quiet and rest, the freedom of mind and body, the close sympathy of his old warhorse, and the beauties of nature which are to be seen at every turn in the mountains of Virginia.

Lee took **Traveller** to the blacksmith and stood by him during the ordeal. He would advise Lexington farrier James Madison Senseney, as he soothed his horse. "He was made nervous by the bursting of bombs around him during the war," Lee explained.

General Lee wrote to Captain Lee on April 25, 1868:

> I have not been as well this winter as usual, and have been confined of late. I have taken up **Traveller**, however, who is as rough as a bear, and have had two or three rides on him, in the mud, which I think has benefited me.

The college had built a new house adjoining the old one. **Traveller** and **Lucy Long** shared a new stable which was described as warm and sunny. The General told an acquaintance "it was a great comfort to know that his horse . . . was under the same roof with himself."

7

THE END OF THE TRAIL

Lee's affection for **Traveller** was in a category by itself, but he was considerate of all animal life. When a hillside forest near Lexington caught fire and burned throughout a winter night, an acquaintance pointed out to Lee the beauty of the scene. Lee responded that it was indeed beautiful, "but I have been thinking of the poor animals which must be perishing in the flames."

When his milk cow died, he mourned her, saying, "I hope that we did our duty to her." He playfully teased his daughter, Mildred, about her pet chickens and her numerous cats, but he allowed her to keep them.

In the heavy firing of the opening Battle of the Wilderness, a courier who dashed up to Lee with a dispatch was startled to get a scolding for having mistreated his horse by riding so swiftly. Lee then took a buttered biscuit from his saddlebag, and fed the hungry animal before turning his attention to the battle.

Still, no animal ever stood as high in his affections as **Traveller**. In a letter to Markie Williams, he expressed his sorrow that a mutual acquaintance, a child, was ill. He added:

"Tell her she must get well and come see my cat, Tom Nipper. He has been reared in the stable, having the advantage of **Traveller's** company, and has acquired the most refined manners."

1925 Stone mountain memorial coin

Lee held dogs in less esteem in his later years than he had in his younger days. Toward the end of his life, however, when he could no longer ride **Traveller**, he wanted a dog who "ought not to be too old to contract a friendship for me." Less than a month after making that statement, Lee was dead.

DECLINING YEARS

As photographs of Robert E. Lee prove, the five years in Lexington were years of gradual physical, although not mental, decline. The heart disease that ultimately killed him, took its toll. By 1869, his afternoon rides on **Traveller** were shorter and less frequent. In December of that year he admitted to his son, Fitzhugh, that "**Traveller's** trot is harder to me than it used to be, and it fatigues me."

Two months later, however, Lee wrote his daughter, Mildred, who was visiting in Richmond:

> I am getting better, I hope, and feel stronger that I did, but I cannot walk much farther than to the college, though when I get on my horse I can ride with comfort.

In May, 1870, he was in Richmond at the request of his doctors. While there, he wrote to his daughter in Lexington and stated, among other things: "I hope that **Traveller** is enjoying himself." In August of that year, he wrote to Mary from Hot Springs in Bath County, Virginia, expressing relief that the family's cow was recovering from an illness (the cow died later that month). In the letter, he said: "She stands next in my affections to **Traveller**. . . ."

A lengthy tour of the deep south in the spring of 1870 and a sojourn at the springs improved Lee's condition only superficially. He was in Lexington for the opening of the college session in September, and many thought his health had improved.

On Wednesday, September 28, 1870, his heart condition, linked with other complications, forced him to bed. In the morning he was fully occupied with correspondence and other tasks relating to the office of President of Washington College. He declined offers of assistance from members of the faculty, whose services he sometimes used. After dinner that day, he attended a four o'clock vestry-meeting of Grace Episcopal Church. The afternoon was chilly and wet, and a steady rain had set in. It didn't stop until it resulted in a great flood, the most memorable and destructive in the region for 100 years.

The church was cold and damp; and General Lee, during the meeting, sat in a pew with his military cape loosely about him. He took part in a conversation that occupied the brief space preceding the call to order. He told, with marked cheerfulness of manner and kindliness of tone, some pleasant anecdotes about Bishop Meade and Chief Justice Marshall.

The meeting was long, and lasted until after seven o'clock. The discussion concerned the rebuilding of the chuch edifice and an increase of the rector's salary. General Lee was chairman, and after hearing all that was said, gave his own opinion briefly and without argument.

A Sense of Duty

He closed the meeting with a characteristic act. The amount required for the minister's salary still lacked a sum much greater than General Lee's portion of the subscription. (His portion was determined by his frequent and generous contributions to the church and to other charities).

When the treasurer announced the amount of the deficit still remaining, General Lee said in a low tone "I will give that sum."

He had seemed tired toward the close of the meeting, and someone remarked that he showed an unusual flush; but at the time no one felt any apprehensions about his health. General Lee returned to his house. Finding his family waiting tea for him, he took his place at the table. He stood to say grace. The effort was in vain, however; his lips could not utter the prayer of his heart.

Finding himself unable to speak, Lee took his seat quietly, without agitation. His face seemed to some of the anxious group about him to wear a look of sublime resignation. He seemed to evince full knowledge that the hour had come when all the cares and anxieties of his crowded life were at an end.

They placed him on a couch, from which he would rise no more. The worst flood in over a hundred years swept through the town of Lexington that night, doing a great deal of damage and carrying off 10 to 15 houses, ruining several warehouses and flooding the canal boat landing.

His family maintained a constant vigil over him and his doctors R.L.Madison and H. T. Barron, attempted to encourage his recovery with medicine and gentle admonishments. Dr. Madison reminded him that he must recover soon because **Traveller** was growing restless in the stable and needed exercise.

The General made no reply, but slowly shook his head and closed his eyes. At one point, those present said, he raised his arm and pointed upward. On October 10, during the afternoon, his pulse became feeble and rapid, and his breathing hurried, with other evidences of great exhaustion. About midnight, he was seized with a shivering from extreme debility, and Doctor Barton felt obliged to announce the danger to the family.

On October 11, he was evidently sinking. His respiration was hurried and his pulse was feeble and rapid. Though less observant, he still recognized whoever approached him; but refused to take anything unless it was prescribed by his physicians. It now became certain that the case was hopeless. His decline was rapid, yet gentle; and soon after nine o'clock, on the morning of October 12, he closed his eyes and his soul passed peacefully from earth.

His last words were believed to be: "Strike the tent," clearly referring to the war years.

After his death, the college trustees rechristen the institution Washington and Lee University and selected Lee's son, George Wasington Custis Lee, to succeed his father as president. **Traveller**, therefore, was allowed to remain in his brick stable. He continued to enjoy the freedom of the Washington and Lee campus, and the Lee family continued to pamper him. With all this, however, the majestic warhorse survived his master by only eight months.

In late June, 1871, Mary Custis Lee, the General's oldest daughter, and her brother Custis, were on the porch of the President's house when **Traveller**, always a priviledged character . . . came browsing around in the yard. **Traveller** was looking for a lump of sugar, and Mary Lee went into the house to fetch it for him. When she returned, she found Custis removing a small nail, or tack, from **Traveller's** foot.

The wound did not bleed, and the horse ate the sugar with relish. In a day or two, however, the hostler reported him unwell, and his illness was diagnosed as tetanus. There were no veterinarians in Lexington, but the same two doctors who had attended Lee in his last days came to look after **Traveller**.

A number of local townspeople and farmers offered suggestions for his care. Mary Lee wrote that everything that skill and devotion could do, was done.

He was given small doses of chloroform. Liquid nourishment was forced down his throat. When he could no longer stand upright, a feather bed was laid on the stable floor to give him all the relief possible, but it was to no avail. Mary Lee wrote:

Poor **Traveller's** groans and cries were heartrending in the extreme, and could be plainly heard in the house. I don't think any of us were able to sleep that last night . . . I am sure we almost felt that we had lost a member of the family.

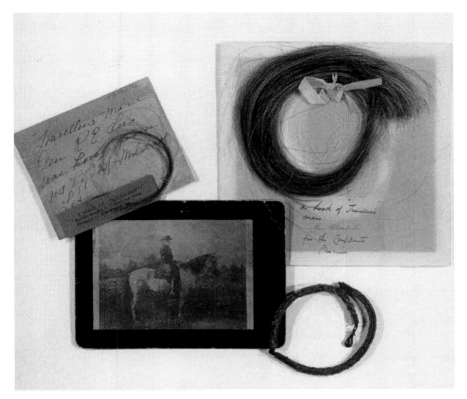

*Locks of **Traveller's** hair and pocket watch chain made of **Traveller's** hair. Photo courtesy of The Museum of the Confederency, Richmond, Virginia*

8

A GOOD PLACE TO REST

Construction began on the University's chapel in 1867 at the request of General Robert E. Lee. The plans were drawn up by Colonel Thomas Williamson and built of brick and native limestone, the chapel was completed in time for graduation exercises in 1868. Lee attended worship services here with the students, and the lower level housed his office, the treasurer's office and the YMCA headquarters. His office remains as he left it for the last time on September 28, 1870.

The morning following his death, the cadets of the Virginia Military Institute escorted his remains from the house to the Washington College Chapel, where they laid in "state" and were guarded by the cadets until the funeral.

> The morning of the obsequies of General Lee broke bright and cheerful over the sorrowful town of Lexington. Toward noon the sun poured down with all the genial warmth of Indian summer, and after mid-day it was hot, though not uncomfortably so. The same solemnity of yesterday reigned supreme, with the difference, that people came thronging into town, making a mournful scene of bustle.
>
> The gloomy faces, the comparative silence, the badges and emblems of mourning that everywhere met the eye, and the noiseless, strict decorum which was observed, told how universal and deep were the love and veneration of the people for the illustrous dead. Everyone uniformly and religously wore the emblematic crape, even to the women and children, who were crowding to the college chapel with

wreaths of flowers fringed with mourning. All sorrowfully and religiously paid their last tributes of respect and affection to the great dead, and none there were who did not feel a just pride in the sad offices.

The scene was peculiarly sad immediately in front of the chapel. All around, the buildings were gloomily draped in mourning and the students strolled listlessly over the grounds, awaiting the formation of the funeral procession.

Ladies thronged about the chapel with tearful eyes, children wept outright, every face wore a saddened expression, while the solemn tolling of the church-bells rendered the scene still more one of grandeur and gloom. The bells of the churches joined in the mournful requiem.

At ten o'clock precisely, in accordance with the program agreed upon, the students, numbering four hundred, formed in front and to the right of the chapel. To the left an escort of honor, numbering some three hundred ex–officers and soldiers, was formed, at the head of which, near the southwestern entrance to the grounds, was the Institute band.

Between these two bodies—the soldiers and the students—stood the hearse and the gray war-steed of the dead hero, both draped in the mourning. The marshals of the procession, twenty-one in number, wore spotless white sashes, tied at the waist and shoulders with crape, and carrying batons also enveloped in the same emblematic material.

Shortly after ten, at a signal from the Chief Marshal, the solemn cortege moved off to the music of a mournful dirge. General Bradley Johnson headed the escort of officers and soldiers, with Colone Charles T. Venable and Colonel Walters H. Taylor, both former assistant adjutant-generals on the staff of the lamented dead.

The physicians of General Lee and the faculty of the college fell in immediately behind the hears, the students following. Slowly and solemnly the procession moved from the college grounds down Washington Street to Jefferson, up Jefferson Street to Franklin Hall, thence to Main Street, where they were joined by a committee of Legislature, dignitaries of the State, and the citizens generally.

Moving still onward, this grand funeral pageant, which had now assumed gigantic proportions, extending nearly a mile in length, soon reached the northeaster extremity of the town, when it took the road to the Virginia Military Institute.

Here the scene was highly impressive and imposing. In front of the Institute the battalion of cadets, three hundred in number, were drawn up in line, wearing their gray uniform, with badges of mourning, and having on all their equipments and side-arms, but without their muskets. Spectators thronged the entire line of the procession, gazing sadly as it wended its way, and the sites around the Institute were crowded.

As the cortege entered the Institute grounds a salute of artillery thundered its arrival, and reverberated far across the distant hills and valleys of Virginia, awakening echoes which have been hushed since Lee manfully gave up the struggle of the "lost cause" at Appomatox.

Winding along the indicated route toward the grounds of Washington College, the procession slowly moved past the Institute, and when the warhorse and hearse of the dead chieftain came in front of the battalion of cadets, they uncovered their heads as a salute of reverence and respect, which was promptly followed by the spectators.

When this was concluded, the visitors and Faculty of the Institute joined the procession, and the battalion of cadets filed into the line in order, with great precision.

After the first salute, a gun was fired every three minutes. Moving still to the sound of martial music, in honor of the dead, the procession reentered the grounds of Washington College by the northeastern gate, and halted in front of the chapel. Then followed an imposing ceremony.

The cadets of the Institute were detached from the line, and marched in double file into the chapel up one of the aisles, past the remains of the illustrious dead, which lay in state on the rostrum, down the other aisle and out of the church. The students of Washington College followed next, passing with bowed heads before the mortal remains of him they revered and loved so much, and well as their president and friend.

ORDER OF THE PROCESSION

Escort of Honor – consisting of Officers and Soldiers of
the Confederate Army

Chaplain and other Clergy

Hearse and Pall-bearers

Traveller

The Attending Physicians

Trustees and Faculty of Washington College

Dignitaries of the State of Virginia

Visitors and Faculty of the Virginia Military Institute

Other *Representative Bodies* and *Distinguished Visitors*

Alumni of Washington College

Citizens

Cadets of Virginia Military Institute

Guard of Honor – Students of
Washington College

The side aisles and galleries were crowded with ladies. Em-
blems of mourning met the eye on all sides and feminine

affection had hung garlands of flowers on all the pillars and walls.

The central pews were filled with the escort of honor, composed of former Confederate soldiers from this and adjoining counties, while the spacious platform was crowded with the trustees, faculties, clergy, legislative committee and distinguished visitors.

Within and without the consecrated hall the scene was alike imposing. The blue mountains of Virginia, towering in the near horizon; the lovely village of Lexington, sleeping in the calm, unruffled air, and the softened autumn sunlight; the vast assemblage, mute and sorrowful; the tolling bells and pealing cannon, and the solemn words of the funeral service—these all combined to render the scene one never to be forgotten.

The sons of General Lee, W. H. F. Lee, G. W. C. Lee, and Robert E. Lee, Jr.; with their sisters, Misses Agnes and Mildred Lee; and the nephews of the dead, Fitzhugh, Henry C., and Robert C. Lee, entered the church with bowed heads, and silently took seats in front of the rostrum.

Then followed the impressive funeral services of the Episcopal Church for the dead, amid a silence and solemnity that was imposing and sublimely grand.

There was no funeral oration, in compliance with the expressed wish of the distinguished dead; and at the conclusion of the services in the chapel, the vast congregation went out and mingled with the crowd outside who were unable to gain admission.

The coffin was then carried by the pallbearers to the library room, in the basement of the chapel, where it was lowered into the vault prepared for its reception. The funeral services were concluded in the open air by prayer, and the singing of General Lee's favorite hymn.

Following the death of **Traveller**, the Lexington Gazette reported a simple five-line obituary. **Traveller** was buried in the ravine cut by Wood's Creek behind the main buildings at Washington and Lee University.

Writing in 1929 to dispel the myth that **Traveller's** remains had simply been pushed over a cliff, Margaret Letcher Showell of Lexington stated that eight people had attended the burial: Custis Lee; four girls, including herself; and three men who assisted in burying the horse.

Traveller was dragged to a grave that had been lined with planking. The carcass was covered with lime, and Custis Lee spread the warhorses's blanket over him before a wooden lid was fitted over the grave.

No one spoke a word at the burial, Margaret Showell said, and emphasized she would never forget the tender grimness of General Custis Lee's face as he stood with bared head beside the grave.

Writing a few years earlier than Margaret Showell, Hunter McDonald, who grew up in Lexington, recalled that a number of young boys from the town had attended the burial, and that **Traveller's** grave was near their swimming hole. He wrote:

> It was our habit, when warming up on shore after a plunge in the cold water, to pay a visit to **Traveller's** grave, but I confess that we were attracted more by the possibility of discovering his bones, unearthed by dogs, than by any attempt to pay our respects to his memory.

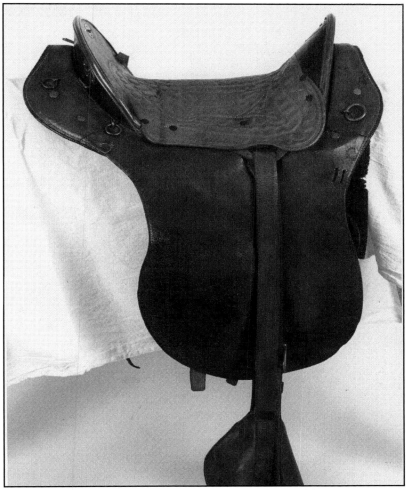

Traveller's saddle. Photo courtesy of the Museum of the Confederacy

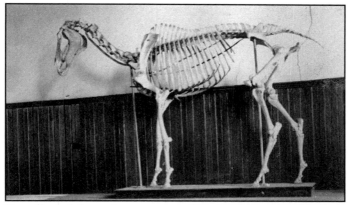

Traveller's skeleton photo courtesy of Washington and Lee University

9

HIS SPIRIT REMAINS

Traveller did not rest long in his grave, but his bones were not "unearthed by dogs." Legend has it that ne'er-do-wells, prompted by a prominent Richmond businessman, dug up the bones in 1876 for display at the Centennial Exposition in Philadelphia.

Some say it happened in 1893, for the Columbian Exposition in Chicago. Still others claim it was in 1907 for the Jamestown Exposition in Norfolk. The years and expositions differ, depending on who tells the tale.

They intended to make a bundle of money from this ignoble deed, but were apprehended, the story goes. Rather than return the bones to their resting place, officials at Washington and Lee had the skeleton mounted and placed on display in the university's museum.

As with most legends, this one contains elements of truth. A prominent Richmond businessman did have the bones mounted in 1907, and they were placed on display at the university. No satisfactory evidence has come to light yet that can explain exactly who had the bones dug, or when or why.

Traveller's bones were definitely out of the ground by 1875, and their disinterment may have been related to an anonymous gift of $25,000 that Washington and Lee received that year. The gift, to be used to establish a museum of geology and natural history, was transmitted through Professor Henry A. Ward, of Rochester, New York.

Professor Ward was an imminent museologist whom the donor also designated to collect and arrange specimens for display. Stuffed animals and mounted skeletons were to comprise the zoological section of the museum.

Curtis Lee and Henry Ward corresponded about the museum, and it is possible that the idea of displaying **Traveller's** skeleton as an example of equine anatomy was Curtis Lee's.

STILL TRAVELING

On November 28, 1875, Henry Ward requested of Curtis Lee:

> Please ask Professor Richard S. McCulloch, McCormick Professor of Experimental Philosophy and Practical Mechanics at Washington and Lee and directly involved in setting up the museum, to bring me along, as freight, the bones of **Traveller,** I enclose the tags for the box.

Traveller's bones were taken to Rochester, New York, for bleaching and mounting. On July 2, 1877, Ward wrote Lee "that the bones of **Traveller,**" by reason of some treatment at the outset before they came into my hands, were stained so deeply red that I have ... been quite unable to bleach them."

Ward had tried for a year to remove the stain, and because he had failed, he did not assemble the skeleton for display. Henry Ward lived unto 1906, but apparently had nothing else to do with **Traveller's** bones.

In 1907, the 100th anniversary of Robert E. Lee's birth may have rekindled an interest in **Traveller's** skeleton. That spring, the *Lexington Gazette* announced that **Traveller's** bones would soon be mounted. On October 2, the *Gazette* reported that **Traveller's** skeleton had arrived in Lexington from Rochester.

The article also noted that **Traveller** had been "buried in a box back of the college, and later the bones were taken up and preserved for many years. The article gave no clue, however, as to where the bones had spent the 30 years between their shipment to Rochester in 1873 or 1876, and their return to Lexington, mounted, in 1907. All that is known is that Joseph Bryan, a prominent Richmond newspaper man, paid $97.26 to have the bones mounted.

When the identity of the anonymous donor, Lewis Brooks, became known after his death in 1877, the biological and geological museum at the university was named the Brooks Museum. Since a proposed Lee museum had not been completed by 1907, University officials placed **Traveller's** skeleton on display in the Brooks Museum in the northeast wing of the old Washington College building.

The red stain that Henry Ward had observed in 1877 was never removed from the bones after the skeleton went on display, it suffered additional staining, as well as some mutilation.

Fun With Traveller

To several student generations at Washington and Lee, **Traveller** became a symbol of good luck in passing an examination or a course. They had the notion that carving or writing their initials on **Traveller's** bones was insurance against flunking, so ink stains joined the unidentified red stains, and these were set off with incised initials.

It is not a surprising revelation to learn that little change was noticed in the pass-fail statistics when the university administration ended this custom. They ended it by placing **Traveller's** skeleton in a glass case.

Ironically, **Traveller's** physical location within the museum spawned other nonsense. He was placed next to the skeleton of a colt; although some say it was a goat, and others say it was a plastic model of a prehistoric horse's skeleton.

Guides taking visitors through the Brooks Museum some-times pointed to the smaller skeleton and informed their guests that it was **Traveller** as a colt, while the larger skeleton was **Traveller** after he had grown up. A longtime Lexington resident remembered that "hardly anybody found it the least bit silly or frightening that **Traveller** should have had two skeletons."

From the time **Traveller's** bones went on display in 1907, a rumor persisted that the skeleton was actually that of another horse. Other horses had been buried in a ravine behind the Washington and Lee campus, but it seems unlikely that Curtis Lee would have identified the wrong skeleton as **Traveller.**

Considering Henry Ward's meticulous manner in handling and labeling specimens, it is also unlikely that the bones were confused with those of another equine while they were in *his* custody. Washington and Lee students were aware of the rumors, and in 1940 it became the basis of a skillfully written hoax that appeared in the *Southern Collegian,* a student publication.

According to this account, not only were the bones not **Traveller's,** they were the bones of **Cascade,** a horse purportedly once owned by Ulysses S. Grant. In a well-planned scheme, the story went, a northerner living in Lexington in the 1870s substituted the bones of General Grant's horse for those of General Lee's. Thus it was **Cascade's** skeleton, not **Traveller's,** that became "an almost sacred possession of the South."

The Brooks Museum was dismantled in 1936, but sometime before the autumn of 1929, **Traveller** was moved to the Lee Museum in the basement of Lee Chapel on the campus of Washington and Lee. Here he stood on display for more than 30 years, as his bones turned darker and the apparatus of his mounting began to give way.

When the structural elements of the chapel under whose roof he stood began to show the effects of time, it became apparent that both **Traveller** and the chapel needed attention. In the early 1960s, Washington and Lee undertook a major renovation and restoration of the chapel. It and the museum were closed to the public, and **Traveller** was secreted away into storage.

The restoration of the chapel turned out well, but **Traveller's** bones were so badly deteriorated that little could be done for them. Instead of returning the skeleton to public view, it was decided that **Traveller** should be re-interred.

The skeleton, enclosed in a wooden box and encased in concrete, was buried on the front campus, just outside the Lee Chapel and only a few yards from his master's tomb.

THE SPIRIT OF TRAVELLER

It is said that the spirit of **Traveller** still roams the grounds of Washington and Lee University. Students, faculty and visitors have reported hearing the trot of hooves and smelling the scent of a horse when there is no one present. The doors to his stable are never closed, in the hopes his spirit can come and go as he wishes-just like in the old days.

From the piles of pennies I have observed on his grave, students still hope **Traveller** will grant them safe passage in their pursuit of an education. Sure, and horses love apples!

When Grant and Lee met at Appomattox to discuss the terms of surrender, this was the beginning of the end of the hostilities of the Civil War. **Traveller** delivered Lee to the McLean house, and was turned out onto the lawn to indulge himself of the new spring grass.

Grant arrived on his horse, **Cincinnatie.** He, too, was turned out onto the lawn, and began enjoying the same grass. Neither horse minded the other, and there was plenty for both.

Perhaps this great country could learn a lot from these two horses. Through the horrors of war and the good times spent on long rides in the mountains of Virginia, **General Lee and Traveller** shared sweet confidence. It is evident that they were cemented together in a strong bond.

It is also fair to say that we are but spectators to that bond, and can never penetrate their mutual affection. When thinking of a bond this firm, I am reminded of the phrase, "If you have to ask, you would not understand." Some people will never understand or appreciate the ability animals have to make our lives better.

It is even harder to prove with any confidence that we know the thoughts of any animal. Nonetheless, all animals have personalities. Anyone who has ever loved a pet can attest to this fact. From time to time, one of these personalities stands out as a favorite.

A Word for the Rest of Us

What does the intriguing account of **Traveller** mean to the rest of us. What are some of the lessons we learn, the voices we hear in this fascinating story?

1. An explicable bond of understanding and spirit can exist between humans and animals that defies the human vocabulary. This kind of relationship existed between General Robert E. Lee and his war-horse, **Traveller.** This was obvious to those who were around them for any length of time.

2. After more than a century since those years of pain and heartbreak for our beloved nation, conflict, unfortunately, is still a part of the human condition.

3. The continued building of our nation and the guarding of our freedoms remain an imperative and costly enterprise that requires constant vigilance and, often, sacrifices from all of us.

4. The triumphant spirit of the moral and godly will ultimately prevail, regardless of which side of history one is on.

5. We must work for understanding and generosity as we treasure every creature in all of God's creation.

So, we conclude this story of **Traveller.** This is about all we know about him. Although he was only a horse, for many of us he was a hero and an inspiration. His life was significant because he did his duty well.

Who of us would not like to have a friend and be a friend like **Traveller?**

Photo courtesy of Washington and Lee University

"The Soldiers' Tribute" by Don Troiani

ADDENDA

ROBERT E. LEE TIMELINE

1807

- JANUARY 19, Robert E. Lee is born at Stratford Hall in Westmoreland County, VA.

- Lee's father "Light-Horse Harry Lee" was a hero of the American Revolution and a friend of George Washington.

1829

- Lee graduates second in his West Point class.

- He graduates without a single demerit.

- Fellow cadets give Lee the nickname "Marble Statue."

- He is commissioned a second lieutenant in the U.S. Corps of Engineers.

1831

- Lee marries Mary Custis (granddaughter of George and Martha Washington) at Arlington House, her family's plantation.

- The Lees have seven children during their marriage.

1846

- The Mexican War begins.

1847

- Lee, promoted to brevet major, serves on General Winfield Scott's staff.

1852

- Lee becomes superintendent of the United States Military Academy at West Point.

1859

- October 18, Lee leads troops in putting down John Brown's raid on Harpers Ferry.

1861

- April, General Winfield Scott offers Lee command of the Union Army

- April 17, The Virginia convention votes in favor of secession.

- April 22, Lee resigns from the United States Army.

- Lee accepts command of the military and naval forces of Virginia.

- Virginia military forces become a part of the Confederate forces.

- Lee is sent to defend western Virginia.

- Lee is called to Richmond to serve as a military advisor to President Davis.

- July 21, Battle of Bull Run

1862

- Lee purchases his famous warhorse, **Traveller**.

- March, The Peninsular Campaign begins

- June 1, Lee is given command of the Army of Northern Virginia after General Joseph E. Johnston is wounded.

- June, the Battle of Seven Pines, sometimes called Fair Oaks.

- June 26-July 2, 1862, the Seven Days Battles

- August 29, 30, 1862, Battle of Second Bull Run in Northern Virginia

- September 1862, Battle of Antietam in the state of Maryland

1863

- May, the Battle of Chancellorsville in Virginia

- July, the Battle of Gettysburg in Pennysvania.

1864

- May 8-21, the Battle of Spottsylvania in Virginia

- June, the Battle of Cold Harbor in Virginia

- June, the Seige of Petersburg, Virginia, begins

- The first steps in turning Lee's plantation home into a national cemetery occurs when Union soldiers are buried on the property.

1865

- January 1, Lee is made general-in-chief of Confederate Forces.

- April 2, The siege of Petersburg ends when Grant attacks Lee's position.

- April 9, Lee surrenders to Grant at Appomattox Courthouse, Virginia.

- April 10, Lee issues his Farewell Address to the Army of Northern Virginia.

- October, Lee becomes president of Washington College in Lexington, Virginia.

1870

- October 12, General Robert E. Lee dies after suffering a stroke at age 63.

1871

- June, **Traveller**, Lee's favorite warhorse, dies.

FAMOUS CIVIL WAR HORSES

CONFEDERATE MOUNTS

♦   **Fleeter** was the horse of *Belle Boyd,* a famous Confederate spy.

♦   **Black Hawk** was the horse of *Major General William B. Bate.*

♦   **Dixie**, the battle steed of *Major General Patrick R. Cleburne,* was killed in battle at Perryville.

♦ **Rifle** was the much-cherished steed of *Lieutenant General Richard S. Ewell.*

♦ **King Phillip** was ridden by *General Nathan Bedford Forrest.* He also owned and rode **Roderick** and **Highlander.**

♦ **Beauregard** was ridden to Appomattox by *Captain W.I. Raisin.* He survived until 1883.

♦ **Old Sorrel,** formerly a Union officer's mount, was acquired by *General Stonewall Jackson* at Harper's Ferry when she was about 11 years old. The mare was so small that Jackson's feet nearly dragged the ground, so she came to be called **Little Sorrel.** He was riding **Little Sorrel** when he was mortally wounded.

♦ **Joe Smith** was the name of the horse ridden by the *Brigadier General Adam R. Johnson.*

♦ **Fire-Eater** was a splendid bay thoroughbred ridden by *General Albert S. Johnston* when he was killed at Shiloh.

◆ **Nellie Gray,** a mare ridden by *Major General Fitzhugh Lee*, the General's nephew, was killed in the Battle of Opequon in the Shenandoah Valley.

◆ **Old Fox** was ridden by *Colonel E.G. Skinner* of the First Virginia Infantry.

◆ **Virginia** is said to have prevented the capture of *Major General J.E.B. Stuart* by jumping an enormous ditch.

"Picketts Charge" Gettysburg National Park

♦ **Highfly** is the name of another horse *General Stuart* rode frequently.

♦ **Sardanapalus** was the favorite mount of *M. Jeff Thompson,* a Confederate partisan of Missouri.

UNION MOUNTS

Old Whitey was the name of the usual mount ridden by *Mother Bickerdyke,* a famous female nurse.

Almond Eye was the name of the steed ridden by *Major General Benjamin E. Butler.*

Methuselah was the name of the white horse *Colonel Grant* rode into Springfield, Illinois, in 1862.

Cincinnatie was a gift to *Lieutenant-General U. S. Grant,* and was quickly recognized as his favorite horse. Grant first rode into battle on the back of **Rondy**, and during the war also used **Fox, Jack, Jeff Davis** and **Kangaroo.**

Lookout was acquired at Chattanooga by *Major General Joseph Hooker.* Named for a battle of that campaign, **Lookout** stood 17-hands-high, and was cherished by Hooker.

Moscow was a white horse used in battle by *Major General Philip Kearny* against the advice of his colleagues. This may have been his favorite. Because the big horse was an inviting target, Kearny switched to a bay named **Decatur,** and then to **Bayard**, a light brown horse.

Slasher was ridden into battle by *Major General John A. Logan,* and depicted by an artist in a famous picture as dashing along a line of battle with all four feet off the ground.

Boomerang was the warhorse of *Colonel John McArthur* of the Twelfth Illinois Regiment. He acquired his name because of his tendency to move backward.

Kentuck was probably the favorite mount of *Major General George B. McClellan. McClellan* also rode a black horse named **Bums.**

Baldy, ridden by *Brigadier General George G. Meade,* was wounded at First Bull Run and at Antietam. This horse later took Meade to Gettysburg where both the horse and master received a promotion. Philadelphia's Old Baldy Civil War Round Table helps to commemorate the memory of this horse.

Aldebaron was an early mount of *Colonel Philip Sheridan.* He later gave way to a gelding named **Rienzi**. After a famous ride to **Winchester,** the name of the animal was changed to that of the town. **Winchester** was so revered that when he died, his stuffed body was presented to the Smithsonian Institution.

Lexington was *General William T Shermar's* favorite mount. He also rode **Dolly** and **Sam**.